New Era, Old Love

Sloan Solarin

SS

ARTWORK CREDIT: DANIELLE MURRELL COX–
WWW.DMCMTL.COM

Inspired by true events.

A story about a boy
a *girl*
and a few lessons
about a thing called love.

Foreword

At first, I didn't want to. Next, I couldn't figure out how. But in some way, shape or form, I didn't always believe in love.

I didn't know what it was. It seemed to exist only in storybooks and on television screens.
Life in the real world couldn't allow for something so seemingly ridiculous to be of any substance, at least not for very long.

What about divorce rates?
What about lies? What about affairs?
What about loneliness, sadness, death and heartache?
Or even worse, death *by* heartbreak.
The numbers didn't add up.

At best, it was an ever-elusive concept—an ideal that no matter how far pursued, remained out of reach.

But feeling is believing.
My questions and perceptions of love were ill-founded.
Maybe I was afraid of its transformative power.

I may not have been ready. Let me be the first to confess to you; I was wrong about love.
It's real. It's necessary.
It's beautiful.

Chapter 1: Still Waters

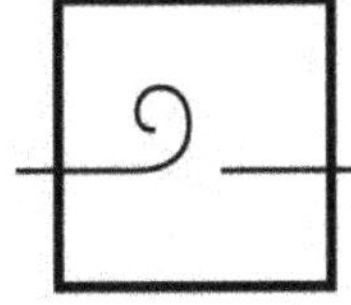

1.1

[Of Heart & Mind]

The very best lovers, the ones who seemingly compel us to feel, whom we miss whether near or far, are the ones with bleeding hearts, and rock-solid convictions.

1.2

[Sorcery]

It's more than support,
vulnerability, inspiration,
acceptance, passion, and maybe even
life itself. It's beyond the meeting
of devotion and otherworldly
affection. It's levels above when
another's touch feels better than
the richest, softest fabric.
I can tell you without hesitation,
it's greater than reason, logic or
any science can justify. Love.

1.3

[A Story Untold]

I daydreamed of blank pages, ready
to be filled with stories of us.
We'd build an empire for two, to
last an eternity.
I'd keep her with me forever,
anywhere and everywhere, through
anything and everything, until the
Sun set on our dying days.

With her fingers locked between
mine, I'd hold her, through the
tears, the fears, the hardships and
the years.

In matters of the heart, mine had
always belonged to her, and so I
wished it would remain.

1.4

[Heart Speak]

What was I supposed to do? The words were too small, and the languages of the world were too few. But it wasn't vocabulary, or the lack thereof. Maybe the feelings were too real, too raw, too new, too … true. And each and every time, everything I felt was for you.

1.5

[Below Sea Level]

She didn't want a storybook love. She left her ideas of fairy-tale romance in the pages of her childhood. Gone was her interest in over-the-top theatricality. What she hoped to find was simplicity and honesty, as consistent and calm as the waves of a low tide, with the depth of the deepest ocean.

1.6

[Magic Dust]

Once upon a time, I too felt
unworthy, unwanted—unloved.
No matter how high I climbed, I fell
short. My friends thought I expected
too much, and that my personality
was too difficult. Unwilling to
compromise my standards, through
teary eyes and clasped hands, I
begged the universe to make me
enough. Then out of the blue, *I* met
her, and *we*, became *us*: 2 parts
magic, equal parts lust, a sprinkle
of havoc, and unwavering trust.

1.7

[20/Twenty]

Most of us don't see each other
clearly. But she saw *me*—the real me,
with every kink in my armor exposed:
all of my layers, no facades,
falling apart, yet put-together.
Her vision was so clear that she
reached out to feel me. And in that
moment, I saw a future for us.

We'd go back in time, to find a
stubborn, hard-working, everlasting
passion—old love in a new era.

1.8

[Smooth Seas]

To her, I smiled for no apparent
reason. Unbeknownst to her, *she* was
the reason. She taught me lessons I
couldn't previously grasp.
I learned that things could be
beautifully simple, honest, and
easy. Too easy.

We grew so accustomed to the
smoothness of our sea that we hadn't
prepared for the coming storms.
A drizzle could turn into a pouring
rain. And the storms, unabashedly,
they always came.

1.9

[Uncommon Sense]

Is it possible to live and love
without the possibility of
heartbreak? I honestly don't think
so. Not unless you trade love for
the utmost caution.
But then, that wouldn't be *love*, now
would it? It would be careful and
commonplace. And that's an uncommon
place for the heart and its
strongest emotion to live.

1.10

[Vicious Cycle]

We met. We loved.
We laughed. We cried.
And though we both would carry on
existing, in the end, *we* died.

Chapter 2: Fool's Gold

2.1

[Sensory Residue]

When she left, I don't think I missed her, at least not as much as the parts of myself I entrusted to her, the parts I could never get back even though I yearned for them so desperately. All that remained was phantom pain.

2.2

[Perspective]

I was weak for her. But strength
allowed me to sink into the deepest,
darkest depths of her being.

She said with me she felt strong.

Yet it was weakness that made me
clutch harder to her, despite the
signs we were no more.

2.3

[Fourth Season]

When the mornings came, I daydreamed
of myself laughing and smiling with
her. She'd be my lifelong summer.
I envisioned a life where age
and time couldn't cause our
affection to wither.

But I, or maybe we, were seemingly,
her coldest winter.

2.4

[Cat & Mouse]

The thought of her fueled me. It
propelled me forward, ever toward
her, but never any closer.
Even as we laid together, side by
side, she was drifting away,
further, and faster than any speed
I could hope to sustain.

It's been said that "Distance makes
the heart grow fonder." Now I
wonder, in this instance, does
distance, make the heart go wander?

2.5

[Introspection]

Somewhere along the line, something changed in her. And I knew we were in trouble. Maybe I didn't make her heart race, maybe I didn't cause her eyes to sparkle. Maybe I didn't give her goosebumps, or leave her awestruck. Maybe I didn't make her feel like the only one in the world. Maybe I wasn't her paradise.

Is that why she did it?

Is that why, while we were being her and I, she was becoming *us* with another lover?

2.6

[Cumulonimbus]

I used to envision so many versions
of the perfect life with her.
But in the blink of an eye,
those very scenes became scars,
blood spatter—dark matter, scattered
across my heart and mind,
like rain clouds on what was once
a clear blue sky.

2.7

[Gift & Curse]

I was a loving child.
My grandmother used to say I was the sweetest little boy in the world—a child with a heart so enormous, mountains paled in comparison.
That same heart brimmed with compassion and consideration.

My biggest gift was also my biggest curse. It felt as though I was born to love, but damned, never to have it returned, with a depth of emotion so profound the very thought of it petrified me and pushed me to extremes that at once built me up and broke me down.

… And if love is king, why all the cracks in my crown?

2.8

[Glitter & Gold]

One day, she too will fall, fast and
far. It's inevitable really.
She'll give her heart, her soul, her
entire being to another. She'll go
to great lengths, past humiliation
and beyond reason to do so.
I hope it lasts. And I hope it's
real—as real as the air in her lungs
and the life in her soul.

At the end of the day, when my story
is told, though to her I was
glitter, to the next I'll be gold.

2.9

[Sustenance]

There may be times when you'll look
around and be suffocated at the
sight of affection, attraction, and
any form of fondness. You'll feel
anger, hurt, and loathing, because
you too will be broken. I'm begging
you, please let it go. It's a hurdle
you need to overcome. Hatred in any
form poisons the heart.
What sustains us, heals us and
ultimately makes us whole, is pure,
unabashed, unrelenting love.

2.10

[Learning Curve]

There's freedom in being left behind—nothing to lose, everything to gain. I no longer want for anything, not a single thing, except for another chance to turn love into my own pièce de résistance. There are no guarantees in love. There's always a risk—one that brought me face to face with my deepest fears.

I know that now. And so, I'm thankful to her for teaching me this lesson. Now I understand that I've never been *enough*, nor will I ever be. I've been, I remain, and I will always be, *more than* enough, for the right one for me.

2.11

[Finite]

There was just her and I.
It was just us.
And we could have been limitless.

Chapter 3: Free Fall

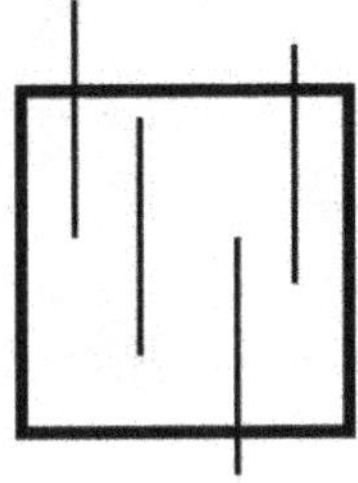

3.1

[Time Capsule]

If I could travel through time,
both past and future, watching as
romances came and went,
seeing hearts ache, break, and
torment. Would there have been, and
could there be, a single living soul
who felt as utterly betrayed and
alone as me?

3.2

[Sub-Zero]

I was frozen in time, searching for purpose, answers, a person to call, anything at all. It was dark, and I couldn't see. In all honesty, I'm not certain I wanted to.

I felt tattered, abused, marred and shattered, confused. I couldn't see the end of the day, let alone look toward the future, a future that once upon a time belonged to us.

3.3

[Growing Pangs]

On some days, it was a little easier
to smile. On other days, I wished I
was a kid again, so my grandmother
could hold my hand to start the day,
caress my face, wipe my tears and
say, "My innocent sweet child,
everything's going to be okay."

3.4

[The Fallen]

I loved her, in every single way I
knew how. So much so, that all these
years later, I still can't find the
words to explain. But for her it was
something entirely different.
For her it was, temporary.
The difference between the two
was almost the death of me.

It was earth shattering.

And when the ground crumbled beneath
me, I began to fall, no longer into
love, but toward rock bottom.

3.5

[Crash Landing]

After what felt like forever and a day, I crashed. I had finally reached my lowest point—so low that the notion of keeping my head up only reminded me of how far I had fallen. This was my life: a series of unfortunate events that played out with intermissions of failed attempts at happiness.

3.6

[Force of Nature]

So, this was the heartbreak they
spoke of. She was gone for good,
yet I remained, wishing, hoping,
praying for her return, even amidst
all the pain.

I suppose I always knew she would
shake me, knock me down, dismantle
my pieces, and break me. The very
moment she walked into my life,
I knew she'd leave, because girls
like her could never stay with boys
like me, at least not for very long.
But she was too much—too beautiful,
too magnetic, too angelic.

I could never give back everything
she had to offer, nor would I
forget. Before long, the truth of
what we both were was clear to see.
She was a gorgeous cyclone, and I
her debris. She left nearly as fast
as she'd abruptly arrived, and in a
matter of moments, I had lived and
loved, but was now barely alive.

But I did survive.

3.7

[All the World's A Stage]

For months, as life passed me by,
I simply existed, finding comfort in
the company of substances and people
I knew very little about,
if anything at all. Until finally,
I gathered the strength to lift my
head. I looked around at all of my
broken parts and had an epiphany.

Now I could rebuild my world, my
life, myself. I could put the pieces
of the puzzle back together and on
display for the universe to see. And
my oh my, how beautiful it would be.

3.8

[Less ≠ More]

It's less about the girl I loved
and more about the millions of ways
I planned to love, again.
I prayed to the stars that it'd all
work out in the end.

3.9

[Tragic]

It's special when someone
thinks of you.
It's magical when someone
cares for you.
It's beautiful when someone
lives for you.
It's powerful when someone
dies for you.
But it's a tragedy that sometimes
that isn't enough.

3.10

[Tunnel Vision]

I needed to see something, anything,
other than these strains and hues,
and shades of greys and the blues.
I may have been wrong to make her my
muse. Or maybe she was never mine at
all, and so she was never mine,
to lose.

Chapter 4: Then There Was HER

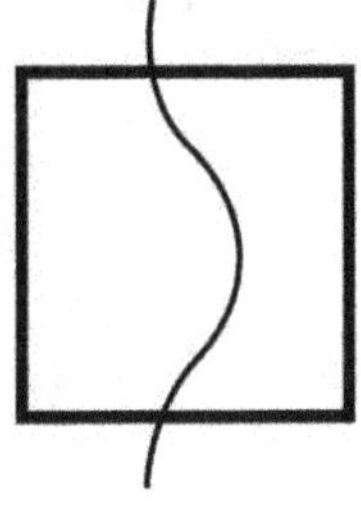

4.1

[A Moment's Notice]

We must've known the instant our
eyes first met—known that ages
before we'd ever met one another,
our paths were fated to cross.
We were quite unlike two strangers
in the night. I was an immovable
object and she was an unstoppable
force. And though we may in fact
have been polar opposites,
we understood each other, better
than anyone else, better than we
understood ourselves.

From that moment on, we belonged to
no one but ourselves and each other.

4.2

[Phoenix]

In her brilliance, her resilience,
her courage, and the sum,
a woman like her
could incinerate the Sun.

4.3

[Moment of Clarity]

All of a sudden, she became clear to
me. Before I knew it, she was all I
could see. She had an aura. She was
different and I could tell, even
from a distance. Unknowingly, she
became my hope, even if at first,
she was just a glimmer of it.
She was unlike me, and I was unlike
her. And together we would be unlike
anything the world had ever seen.

4.4

[Mud Diamond]

I wanted someone to see me, the real me, all of me—with my quirks and inconsistencies. Someone who would look at my scars without flinching, or gasping and turning away. Someone who would trace their fingers along those very scars as though they were works of art, and marvel. Someone who would acknowledge that I was far from perfect, but willing to see me through my growth and progress. Someone who saw my worth, even when I felt worthless. Someone who was patient, so patient the hands of time would look on enviously. Someone who saw a diamond in the rough that had been knocked down and shuffled about, but if treated with care would outshine the millions of stars that lined the night sky.

4.5

[Self-Worth]

For the first time in a long time
I began to see myself.
I was whole again.
I'd experienced sadness, the brink
of madness, and rage.
I had touched the earth.
I had seen the Sun. I had felt the
rain. Not only had I survived, I now
thrived. I was battle-tested.
I was blessed.
Maybe more, nothing less.

4.6

[Lover's Library]

Maybe I'd take my time, thumbing her
down, caressing her corners, taking
heed of her sweet syllables and
beautiful borders.

Maybe I'd judge her by her cover,
a title of four words. What if I
tried to f---inish her? No time for
the foreword. Maybe I'd hold her,
turn her around and slowly run my
fingers down her spine. I wouldn't
stay for long, but in those moments,
she'd be mine.

What if I took her home to keep
after one playful look.
I'd read her over and over.
She'd be my favorite book.

4.7

[The Flutterby Effect]

You've probably never heard of the
Flutterby Effect, have you?

The notion that if two people meet
at the right place, right time, and
under the right circumstances, what
ensues is a chemistry so potent that
it lasts for generations to come.
It feels like a billion butterflies
are floating and fluttering around
in your stomach. Most people call it
love. It sounds far-fetched,
but it isn't, at least not to anyone
who's fallen in it.

4.8

[Once Upon a Time]

'… And they lived happily ever after'. It's not how you start the race, but how you finish, right? Because who doesn't like sunsets and storybook endings? But what about the sunrise and beautiful beginnings? I think we can take it slow. I'll figure out just how to treat you.

'Hi, my name is----nice to meet you.'

4.9

[Face of Fear]

It was easy to see how different
things would be with her.
She terrified me to the point of
near paralysis. I was afraid to say
too much. I was afraid to do too
little. I was afraid of being
inadequate. I was afraid that I
could not love her beyond measure.
Before her, there were plenty of
others. But no fear. No, I was never
scared. Quite the contrary, they
were afraid of me. Whoever thought
people could care too much, or too
intensely? But we're different
together, her and me. We turn around
and face our fears. We never flee.

4.10

[Secrets & Serenades]

There I was again, in a situation that felt familiar, yet entirely different. We were strangers and lifelong companions. She had skeletons and demons, hidden away in some secret place: a corner or crevice barely accessible to even herself. In that sense, we were one and the same.

But it didn't matter. She danced to the rhythm of her own drum, and I appreciated her even more for it. When the time would come, she'd take me to her secret place. I'd learn her lyrics. They'd be heavenly. Until that time, I'd be satisfied with her beautiful bass and melody.

Chapter 5: Zero Gravity

5.1

[Right Side Up]

I think we were both exhausted—tired
of telling our stories only to have
them fall on deaf ears. Exposing
yourself to someone new is hard.
It's always uncharted territory.
Uncertainty can be a heavy burden to
bear, so much so that some people
are forced into submission. They
don't try anymore. For a long time,
I was one of those people.
I didn't want to trust or be
vulnerable.
I was beginning to think I no longer
could. I was ready to accept my
fate. I was resigned to spend the
rest of my life in the absence of
any real substantial feelings of
love. Then *she* came along. She
flipped my entire world upside down.
And I thank her for it.

5.2

[Chemical Reaction]

I wanted to spend the rest of my
life alongside her. Whether I died
abruptly before my time or lived on
seemingly forever didn't matter, as
long as she was there. I needed her
presence and all she had to offer.
She was everything I admired.
She was the oxygen to my fire.

5.3

[A Woman Apart]

She is the most exhilarating, unpredictable woman I've ever met in my entire life. She does only what she wants to do. She couldn't care less about how other people perceive her. Her mere presence presented a thrill. She had quite simply set herself apart from anyone else I had ever encountered.

5.4

[All or Nothing]

When we laughed together, it never
felt foolish. Or maybe it did and we
just didn't care. When we shed tears
together, we never saw weakness.
Instead, we saw vulnerability,
another kind of strength. Together
we could be ourselves in our truest
form: exposed, daring, hopeful,
jaded. We each recognized the risks
we were taking on each other. And
that was okay, because we knew that
risks weren't worth taking if we
weren't going to risk it all. We
left the place where comfort lies,
with love and dreams,
zero compromise.

5.5

[Oxygen]

We'd already done it hundreds of times, with our words, our hands, our eyes and our minds. No one who came before could dare to matter anymore. I didn't know where to put my hands, her stomach, her waist, her hair, her face.

Suddenly silence had fallen: our first kiss. In that moment, there was nowhere else I'd rather be. She brought a part of me back to life, awakening something I could scarcely believe—new dreams, true passion and a renewed joie de vivre.

5.6

[Universal]

She was and remains inexplicable, a
walking anomaly. I knew she was far
from ordinary. But once I truly
began to understand her, I realized
she was the universe. She made the
extraordinary appear to be extra
ordinary. She was sincere and wild,
from her hair to her smile.
She was brave and smart. No one knew
what she'd do next. And come to
think of it, that's what I loved
about her the best.

5.7

[Disappearing Act]

I wanted to get to know her, the
real and raw version. No, there was
more to it than that. I *needed* to
learn her, inside and out, like the
laws of my favorite language.
She was my love language. With every
new discovery, it was as though a
physical piece of her vanished, gone
with the wind. Her soul was taking
shape before my very eyes. My senses
were now fine-tuned to her: the
sound of her voice, her scent, touch
and the taste of her lips.
I could feel her aura.

5.8

[Iceberg]

We never truly fall for beauty or
appearances, do we? Yes, we may
yearn for, lust, and become
intensely infatuated by looks.
But it won't last. It can't.
Physical attraction fades; it's
always just a matter of time before
it comes and goes. The feelings that
last, the ones we feed on for
emotional sustenance, run much
deeper, they exist much further
beneath the surface level.
That's where substance resides.
It can sometimes be a dark place,
but it's spectacular nonetheless.

5.9

[Confession]

I've seen the wonders of the world.
I've been to so many different
cities and countries.
But I'm a liar. When people ask me,
'What's your favorite place?' Never
once have I answered that question
truthfully. Why? Because the most
breathtaking place I've ever had the
luxury of being, is with her.
She's the one place I want to visit
over and over and over.
I never get bored.
There are always new discoveries
within her mountains and her seas.
And so, if I may, a moment of
honesty, she's the closest thing to
magic my eyes have ever seen.

5.10

[Lady Luck]

Often times I get carried away, lost
in my own thoughts. I've always been
a bit of a daydreamer. Maybe it's
the continuous curiosity in me, but
I find myself wondering, 'What kind
of saint must I have been in a past
life to be lucky enough to deserve
an angel in this one?' I count my
blessings every chance I get.
It is an honor to know her. There is
no one better than her.
She is phenomenal. Her energy is a
phenomenon. I'm privileged every day
that I'm permitted to care for and
love her. I will place nothing
and no one above her.

Chapter 6: Chipped Armor

6.1

[Pinky Swear]

I don't make promises—never have and
never will. The mere thought of
breaking one makes me uneasy.
That's why I couldn't promise her
perfection, not from me and not for
us. We were bound to argue, fuss and
fight. We're different people.
We each have a past, trust issues,
and other baggage. Truth be told,
that was entirely okay. It may even
have been necessary. But I was
willing to try. I'd give her every
bit of effort I could muster.
I'd try, try again, and try some
more. I'd check my ego. I'd swallow
my pride. I'd do what it took, I'd
listen and learn. And I'd hope for
the same, when it was her turn.

6.2

[Unholy Trinity]

There's something to be said about ego, pride and stubbornness. Ego silences the heart and poisons the soul. Then comes pride, the place where reason, love and humility go to die. And finally, stubbornness, the almighty creator of distance between two people who otherwise care for each other dearly. So, I'll apologize even if I'm not wrong. Please forgive my mistakes: past, present and future. I'll tell you I love you, and that you're a work of art, let's be humble together, not proud and apart.

6.3

[Imperfections]

Even a blind man could see it.
We were and remain lightyears away
from perfection. Riddled with flaws.
Maybe that's what made it all worth
it. The more I got to know her, the
more clearly I could see how much of
a marvelous mess she could be. She
was awkward and clumsy—forgetful
too. But that didn't make her any
less wonderful. In fact, among a
million others, those were some of
my favorite imperfections.
They made her, her, and that made
her perfect, at least to me.

6.4

[Faith in Flaws]

Sometimes the little things are a bigger part of a person's being and story than anyone knows. We all have them, character 'flaws'. Maybe it's a limp, or a stutter. Maybe it's a quick temper or blind faith in any and everyone you meet. And as crazy as it sounds, that's precisely what makes us unique. It's what separates us from each other. They don't make us any less or any more deserving. They make us ourselves. We should appreciate our quirks, the crinkles in our otherwise smooth exteriors. That's the best part of getting to know one another.

6.5

[Unforeseen]

There's something beautiful about
plans that don't come to fruition,
like following a path that trails
off into nothingness, or a recipe
that turns into a complete disaster.
There's something real there.
If you close your eyes and envision
it for long enough, you can almost
reach out and touch it.
Plans that fall through, like broken
promises, have a strange charm to
them. There's character and
adversity there. They make or break
us in a way. They make for the most
interesting stories.
Maybe our past relationships fell
through for a reason. Maybe *we're*
that reason. Who would've thought
that so much right could come out of
things going wrong?
So, take my hand, let's run along.
Let's celebrate our broken plans.

6.6

[She & Herself]

She was real. She didn't look like
the people on TV or in magazines.
She didn't act like a character in
those cliché movies with happy
endings either. Her hair wasn't
always perfect. She wasn't satisfied
with her body. She didn't always
know the perfect words to say.
She started books without finishing
them. She got lost, even while using
GPS. She lost her temper.
She broke down and cried.

But she loved her hair, and she
still walked with confidence.
When she couldn't find the right
words, she'd find the right actions,
or at the very least be silent and
give me space. She found different
books that interested her more.
She got to know the places she got
lost in. She eventually calmed down.
She picked herself up and wiped her
tears away.

She was real. And she owned every
part of herself.

6.7

[Alternate Reality]

Life is simple, but we're complex creatures. We hide what we really feel. We censor our thoughts and words, all in the name of social acceptance. Not her though, not me, not us, not at all. We wore our scars like medals of honor the very first time we met. And together we managed to create our own realm of reality. It's a place where we can be ourselves. No masks, no armor, no walls. It's not always an easy place to exist, but it's our place.
It's not a promise or a guarantee. It's a choice, to be naked, to be vulnerable, to be true, to be you, to be me, to be free.

6.8

[Spoils of War]

It's strange. In a way, I feel resentment toward anyone who's ever hurt her. And in the same breath, I'm eternally grateful for everything she's been through until now. I'm thankful for the trials she's faced because they've turned her into the most precious gem I've ever seen. The tribulations she's faced have turned her into a warrior. She's survived hardships and hurdles along the way almost with a sense of duty.
Within her resilience and power lies beauty. Truly.

6.9

[Choose Wisely]

I didn't wear a cape. I was the furthest thing from a hero. Neither of us had ever needed saving. We'd seen our fair share of wars, so to speak. No, we didn't need each other. There was no dependency. What that meant was we were free—to exist as individuals, to exist together, to wake up every day and choose each other. That kind of choice is special. To choose someone time after time, despite knowing how difficult things may one day be or how dark they can become, that kind of devotion is not only courageous, it's magical.

6.10

[Gemstone]

She's seen a bright blue sky turn to clouds. She's experienced storms. She's been swept up and away by natural disasters. She's been held down by thousands of pounds of pressure and pain. She's been shattered against the rocks. But she survived. She's been weathered and weary, yet she's alive.

What makes her worth her weight in gold, is how she responds when left to die in the cold. She is worthy. She is beautiful. She is brilliant. She is bold.

Chapter 7: Civil War

7.1

[Darkness & Demons]

I was ready and willing to weather
her storms. I was in her corner.
I stood by her side with her hand in
mine as she faced off with her most
dangerous demons. The ones she
called friends, and the ones that
were buried deep, so deep she was
uncertain if they were real or
imagined. I carried her load.
My dreams made room for her
nightmares. I gave her my strength,
because I considered her battles to
be my own. Maybe it was me.
Maybe I wasn't strong enough.
Maybe I underestimated her darkness.
But somewhere along the line,
something changed. We changed.
And I can't be certain if it was for
better or worse.

7.2

[Words & Weapons]

When we fought it was cataclysmic.
We hurled hurtful words, like
daggers aimed at a bullseye pinned
to our hearts. After tempers flared,
feet stamped, then doors slammed.
All that remained was shock, and
despair—the aftermath of seismic
activity. The downside to feeling so
strongly, was that it applied to the
full range of human emotion,
and it was limitless.

7.3

[h2o]

And that's the thing about being in love, it makes you feel as though you're walking on water ... or drowning in it.

7.4

[Inferno]

A fire burned inside her. I could
tell from the sparks and cinders
that flashed in her eyes and tone
when she felt attacked or cornered.
Those flashes told the story of a
love that had once burned as bright
as any flame. A flame that
illuminated a trail of tears,
broken promises and pain.

7.5

[Incomplete]

Our hearts and minds were too willful. Somewhere along the way we were taught to mistake acts of genuine kindness for manipulation and mistreatment. Lessons that were now difficult to unlearn. Look at how little we sometimes gave each other—how little patience, how little credit, how little love. We'd given away the best parts of ourselves to people who did not know our value. We were incomplete, incapable of completely trusting, completely forgiving, or being completely vulnerable.

7.6

[Snow Fall]

If she was a storm, I was an avalanche. Unpredictable, swift and unrelenting. With a demeanor so icy that one piercing look would sometimes leave her petrified, frozen in her tracks, for fear of another barrage. In those moments, she felt entirely alone, abandoned and without help. The feelings she showed, ignored and unreturned. She spoke and was met with silence, forced to navigate the ocean of my feelings without guidance.

I can be a lot to process. Please forgive me, I'm a work in progress.

7.7

[Die Hard]

She accused me of tying strings to the things I gave her. But I never kept tabs. There was no balance owing. I decided that nothing would sway me from gifting her everything I could, for no reason, other than she above all else was most deserving. I suppose it's true what they say, "old habits die hard."

But would her old habits, outlive me? Would they be the death of us?

7.8

[Evolution]

Don't take advantage of me.
And though, my kindness is weakness
for you, please don't take it for
granted. I can't be mad at you.
Actually, I can. I just don't want
to be. I'll never hold things
against you. I won't treat you
differently. I won't seek revenge or
go tit for tat with this and that.

I'll learn though. I'll adapt.
And if you don't beat me to it,
eventually I'll have no choice but
to leave. No, I won't leave you.
I won't leave us.

I'll leave this version of myself to
die. Only the strong survive.

7.9

[Doom & Gloom]

Damaged people make for damaged lovers, and damaged lovers not only damage the hearts of others, they damage their own. Damned and destroyed.

Are we all doomed to be alone?

7.10

[Shades of You]

She was full once, full enough to
fulfill anyone. Overflowing even.
And so, she gave and she gave, as
they took and took more. Until one
day, she looked in the mirror and
saw a hollow shell of the person
she'd been before, someone she'd
never seen before. A shadow of her
former self, withered and brittle.
Treading the razor thin line between
depleted and defeated.

It pained me to hear, and I hate
that it's true.
'I couldn't give you more of me
until you gave yourself
enough of you.'

Chapter 8: Paradise Lost

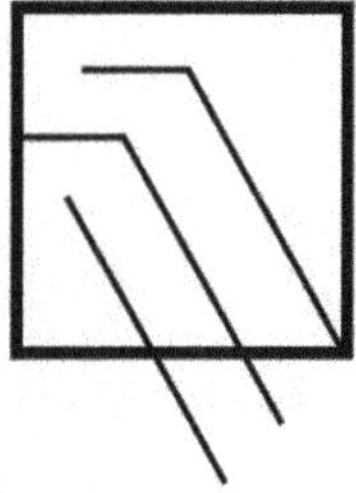

8.1

[Tic Toc]

I hope one day it stops hurting.
I've learned my lesson.
I'm tired of learning.
They say, '*Time heals all wounds,*'
but when it comes to a bleeding
heart, who can say how soon?

8.2

[Fallen Feathers]

And in the blink of an eye,
we were gone. Lost for good.
Was it too much?
Was it too much to ask, to
fearlessly fall into the abyss of
the one who loved her, without
crashing up against the jagged
rocks? Will we ever learn to fall
forever? No crash landing. We spread
our wings. They flutter and flap.
We float and fly, for a while.

Yet somehow, they always
end up broken.

8.3

[Shhh]

It's the quiet pain, that's the one
that hurts most. The one that forces
you to suffer in silence. It seeps
in and suffocates you to the point
where you can't scream, even when
you want to. The kind of hurt that
blinds you, as a soundless stream of
tears trickles down your face.
A noiseless nightmare. This is true
pain, swift and speechless. It will
surround you, in a hushed tone,
leave you weak as a whisper and say,

"You are all alone."

8.4

[Nothingness]

Saying 'goodbye' hurts. But that's only the beginning of it all, isn't it? The next part is where things take a turn for the worst. This is where torture takes over. Now you need to unlearn the lessons that were etched into your heavy heart. You're on your own. You need to fend for yourself—except you're barely alive, and you're empty. All of the mountains, oceans, and stars in the sky can't fill the voracious void inside you. You're slowly becoming a ghost in a shell. A special kind of hell. Your drive is gone. You don't feel like trying. It's hard to live, when you feel like dying.

8.5

[Ground Zero]

There's no beauty or poetry in this
madness. Romance can't exist in a
place where everything your heart
once knew lays in shambles. True
heartbreak is unlike anything you'll
ever see in movies or hear in songs.

It's the memories, of the best
moments of your life, marauding
through your mind saying,
'You'll never be this happy again.'
It's breaking down when you hear
their name or see their friends.
It's crying yourself back to sleep
when you reach over to where they
used to lay, but they're gone now.
There is no silver lining to a pain
so profound, there is only sadness.

8.6

[What's Love?]

It's not enough. Being in love has
never been, and may never be, enough
to keep two people together.
Well, it wasn't for her and I.
There's something to be said about
lovers who feel forced to part ways
while both hearts still beat for
each other. Relationship residue—
so much sorrow.

Because being in love isn't always
being fulfilled. It won't always
mean being appreciated and valued.
It can't protect you or keep you
safe. It doesn't always lead to
happiness and stability.
Sometimes, it's just a 4-letter word
that means you've opened up your
heart to another person.

8.7

[Forgiveness]

I'm sorry my arms weren't strong enough to hold on to you, or even to hold you the way you needed to be held. I apologize for not being tall enough to give you someone to look up to, or to lift you up, onto my shoulders to help you see your way. Forgive me for not being patient enough when you needed time to heal and grow. Sometimes I think it was me who was too much for you, but then maybe it was me who wasn't enough, for you.

8.8

[Supernatural | Super Natural]

I know now that anything is possible. When I died inside, I still kept breathing. You were still alive, and I kept grieving. When I sat in silence, I still kept screaming. My heart was broken, but I kept feeling.

And throughout these nightmares, I still kept dreaming.

8.9

[Little Things]

I want to fall asleep together, even
if we just pressed play. I want to
ask her if she’s eaten, and hear all
about her day. I want to lay in bed
sometimes, and watch her while she’s
getting dressed. I want to finish
all my food, and then help her eat
the rest. I want to rub her neck and
shoulders, run my fingers down her
spine. And hear her ask me all the
questions that she asks me all the
time. I want to wake up, with small
strands of her hair in my bed,
because that’d mean she was here,
and not only in my head.

8.10

[Worth/Less]

For what it's worth, I would've kept arguing. I would've kept trying. I would've kept fighting, because I thought we were worth fighting for. I hope she finds patience and balance. I want her to find love, the way she needs it to be shown, not the way someone else wants to show it. I hope she heals and grows. Grows strong enough to be completely exposed, and vulnerable—vulnerable enough to drop her guard, come down from her tower, and let the next one in without inhibition.

Chapter 9: Pride's Prejudice

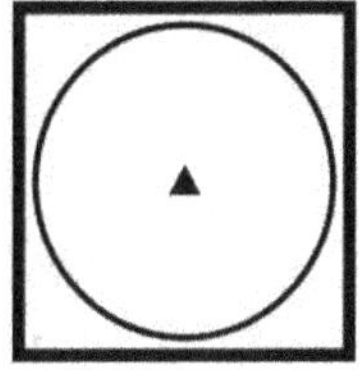

9.1

[Go Seek]

There's no hiding from matters of my own heart. I can't run or escape one painfully simple fact;
I yearn for her.

I miss the way she loved me, and the way she made me feel. She was my strength, my solace, and my savior. She brightened my eyes, put butterflies in my stomach, widened my smile and gave me all of her, even the broken and tattered pieces she sometimes kept out of reach from herself. I needed her. I longed for her. I craved her and the reflection of her I saw in myself. I miss her, and me, and us, both of us.

All of us.

9.2

[Memories of a Future Passed]

She was the beauty in my demise.
She was always more than enough.
I needed her more than I needed me.
I loved her more than I have,
or could ever love me.

Wasn't that terribly, lovely?

She was and remains a masterpiece.
I'd wake up, take one look at her,
and fall right back into her,
and her love.
And on the days that we weren't side
by side, intertwined—a tap, a drum,
a pound, I could feel her heartbeat
from galaxies away.

9.3

[Elements]

On late nights, and early mornings,
I talk to the Moon and stars, the
Sun, and myself. To everyone and no
one in particular, but always about
us. I hope we meet again someday,
when I'm healed and she's back in
one piece. Maybe then, we can become
two full parts of the same whole,
instead of two half parts of one.
If that day ever comes, we'll
compliment and add to one another,
rather than take away.
But until then, I am the quaking
earth beneath her feet, and she's
the brooding storm that sends my
sails off course.

9.4

[What If?]

If I could see the future—if I had
known how things would eventually
play out, I may never have looked
her in the eyes. But she had this
gravitational pull, like nothing I'd
ever seen or felt. Yet here I am,
missing her, wishing I was kissing
her. I may never let her know,
because I need to let her go.
But that's just another secret.
Pride will help me keep it.

9.5

[Bejeweled]

I still want her here, with me. She wasn't perfect, and neither was I. But '*It's the thought that counts*.' Isn't that what they say? We gave it everything we had. Doesn't that count for something? She saw my faults and treasured them, like solid gold. I saw her scars, then kissed and caressed them, longer and harder than any other inch of her beautiful body. Because to me they were diamonds, they made her more than precious, they made her priceless. She was the Sun in my sky, now that she's gone my world is … lifeless.

9.6

[Fleeting Moments]

When my heart forgets, my mind recalls. I remember how much life has to offer. In those moments, I no longer hate the day she left. I no longer search for my reflection in the eyes of another. In those moments, the void is filled and the pain subsides. In those moments, I'm once again alive. I learn to rediscover and redefine myself. I learn to love myself and enjoy my own company. In those moments, I can once again smile, and laugh, go wild and dance. Those moments show me to live *with* love, not in fear of it.

9.7

[Powerful]

She blindsided me. Sharing a world with her was a constant challenge and reward. She forced me out into the open, out of my comfort zone. Because that's where love lives. She made me see the world and myself differently. We experienced so many things. She kept me up at night. And as much as I crave her, I won't go back to her. That would give her power, too much power, enough power to destroy me all over again.

9.8

[Co-Author]

Wherever the wind has taken her,
I still feel her. I hear her
laughter and see her eyes in the
faces of strangers. And though her
absence still hurts, one day I'll be
thankful for what we shared, even
the sad parts, because it's another
chapter in the story of my life,
a chapter authored by her.

9.9

[Heads or Tails]

The truth of the matter is, love,
much like life, just happens.
And the opposite is just as true,
heartbreak, just happens.
It couldn't exist without love,
just like love couldn't exist
without heartbreak, right?
Two sides of the same coin, but a
gamble nevertheless.
Maybe that's why she left.
She did it ever so casually. She was
at war with herself, and I was just
another casualty.

9.10

[Epiphany]

I had an epiphany the other day.
It was never about everything we
felt and put each other through.
It was always about how we
responded, and in turn, what we
decided to do. You reached the
depths of me, that much remains
true. And though you had the best of
me, there's a lot left to me,
without you.

Chapter 10: Freedom. Freedumb. Freedoom.

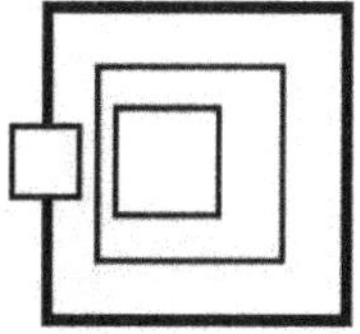

10.1

[Misery Loves]

No one needs company all the time.
But everyone needs company
sometimes. Who that company is isn't
always relevant. We're social
beings. We just need human contact,
companionship—a shoulder to lean on,
an ear to listen, a hand to hold, no
matter how short-lived. We need one
another, to remember what it's like
to love, and laugh, and live, before
the moment escapes us.

10.2

[Darkness Falls]

And so, I search for shelter in
somber spaces: old buildings, dark
alleys and calmer places. Not for
solitude, secrecy or mystery, but
for the simple fact that sometimes,
I think I was created to live my
days and nights on my own, under the
cover of hazily lit lights, alone.

10.3

[Insignificant Other]

On some mornings, you'll wake up
feeling utterly invisible. You'll
still eat and talk, and breathe and
walk. But if you face yourself in
the mirror for long enough,
eventually, you'll blink and fade,
up and away, into obscurity. Because
the one you want to see you the
most, chose not to look your way.
But all's fair in love and war,
and of course pain comes cheap.
It's a different kind of wound,
but it still runs so deep.

10.4

[Metamorphosis]

Sometimes we need change. It may not hurt to be someone new. Not entirely new, but a new and improved version of you. I know that feeling. It's how you feel when you want to be seen; when you don't want to be invisible anymore; when you want to reset and start over. It's the need to let go of the past, to walk away, to leave it all in the rear-view. And that means work—hard work and dedication to being the best version of yourself that you can be. You shouldn't expect anyone to change for you. But you owe change and improvement to yourself. Your well-being is your wealth.

10.5

[Hunger]

Pay attention to those who bleed.
No, not blood, but modesty. The ones
who clothe themselves in honesty.
And honestly, I may never have
realized it myself. Maybe that was
her way of confessing to me, that I
wasn't able to help, at least not
then. She was hungry for more
experience, more wisdom, more of
herself. And even though I did need
her, it was not my time, or place,
or turn, to feed her.

10.6

[Frozen]

I'm familiar with the dark,
and the company of danger,
but the coldest place ever,
is a bed,
in the company of a stranger.
And in those moments,
it becomes quite clear.
There's no waking up if you're
living a nightmare.

10.7

[New Unimproved]

There I was, a "new" me, plagued by
the same plight, feeling cold and
all alone in the dead of a plain
night. And even though I struggled
to find myself, I kept finding
myself in the strangest places.
Where I wished she'd never happened
but hoped she'd happen again.
Where I wrote new endings to a
story, that already had an end.
Where I lived in a place, that I
could not call my home.
Where my heart was in my chest,
but somehow was not my own.

10.8

[Limbo]

In some moments, everything will feel perfect. Your days will get brighter, your heart a little lighter. What lies ahead won't seem so dark. You may even fathom a future where you're genuinely happy. You'll smile at how good and simple life could be.

But every so often, your eyes will wander. You'll see a glimpse of her in someone else, and you'll wonder. What could you have done to get her to stay? You lost your grip, then she slipped away.

10.9

[Shapeshifting]

We may call it different things,
but we all speak the same language.
Don’t we? Grief, sorrow, sadness,
anguish—they’re all the same.
They’re everything we felt, but
didn’t get the chance to show.
They’re the seeds we held, but
didn’t get the chance to sow.
They’re the silent subtle streams
that run down your cheeks. They’re
the thoughts in your head that won’t
let you sleep. Every one of those is
love, just trying to break free.

10.10

[Bad Company]

I thought I could fly, until I
crashed down in the dirt. For what
it's worth, I never thought a human
heart could be this hurt.
I feel marred at all these bars.
I shout and scream at all these
stars, tracing scars, and with every
breath I feel them all.

Are you there? Are you near?
Because this house is not a home.
There's no one here.
And now I'm sleeping all alone.

Chapter 11: Tread Lightly

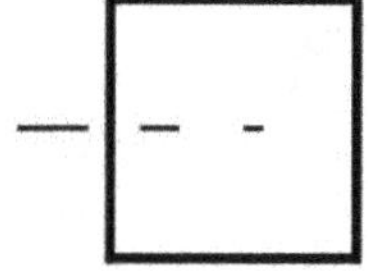

11.1

[Wholesome]

I've always had the pieces of my puzzle. I know that now. She needed to make herself whole again. To be on her own again. To be bare, to be beautiful, to be bold again.

She disappeared and reappeared, much like a warm summer wind,
She sent a message to my phone,
"Hey, how've you been …?"

11.2

[Hiding in Plain Sight]

See, I think there's something
magical, majestic even, hidden in
the devastation of destruction.
Starting anew. Rebuilding, bigger
and better than ever before. There's
bold beauty in beginnings. And to
this, our hearts are no exception.

11.3

[Divinity]

There's a special energy between
two people who've found each other
again, whether for the second,
hundredth or thousandth time.
No distance nor time keeps them
apart. And though their
circumstances may never define
perfection, their fates intertwine,
by divine connection.

11.4

[Seasonal Affectation Disorder]

It wasn't a short wait.
I waited forever for her, through
the fall of the autumn leaves, whose
colors left almost as quickly as she
left me. Through winter nights when
the winds were warmer than the bed I
slept in. Through spring when the
water that wet the ground couldn't
compare to the rain seeking refuge
from my eyes.

But she was the Summer Solstice,
and she was well worth the wait.

11.5

[Ready or Not]

I had to take a step back.
Loving me is no walk in the park.
I didn't realize she wasn't ready to
love me the way I needed to be.
There was no one to blame. Because
what I demanded of her, she owed to
herself: her time, her mind,
her heart—true wealth.

11.6

[Lesson Learned]

Her absence taught me that growth
doesn't always happen in a safe and
stable setting. It doesn't have a
perfect path forward.
We grow in different ways across
unpredictable experiences. I learned
these lessons from her, whether
intentionally or otherwise.
But above all else, being without
her taught me that we must sometimes
burn, and bleed, before we bloom.

11.7

[Boomerang]

She found her way back home.
She found her way back to me.
She apologized, not for what she had
done, not because she had gone, but
because I suffered the consequences
of her actions; her absence.
Where my ego sought revenge, I chose
to forgive instead. I missed her
mind. I missed her shine.
I missed her warmth, in my bed.

11.8

[Risk & Reward]

She stood in front of my palace of peace, struck a match, and set my whole world ablaze. Taking her back wasn't easy. It was quite the opposite. And that's what makes it all worth it.

True love. It isn't always starry eyes and butterflies. Sometimes it's a mess. Sometimes it's patience, acceptance, a lack of pride, and forgiveness.

11.9

[Northern Star]

I was tired of fighting. Fighting to
forgive. Fighting to forget.
Fighting just to live, fighting the
possibility of regret. The truth was
simple. We were writing a story, a
tale of two lovers, and even though
we'd been lost, we were never lost
to each other.

11.10

[End Game]

Just because it ends,
that doesn't mean it's over.

Chapter 12: Moment of Clarity

12.1

[Thank You:]

For your touch.
For your wisdom.
For your courage.
For your strength.
For your compassion.
For your companionship.
For allowing me to be myself.

12.2

[Complete]

I spent what felt like an eternity
looking for the one who I thought
would complete me. Had I taken a
deep breath and a couple of steps
back, I would've realized it was my
job to make myself whole again.
Only then could we complete
and complement each other.

12.3

[Reminder]

In case you needed a reminder,
I need you to know that I love you
with all the energy my heart can
muster. I understand that I'm
privileged to know you, and even
more so to call you my queen. I want
you to know that I am eternally
grateful for your belief in me
and your uplifting words.
I hope you know that as long as you
let me, I will move mountains,
swim the seas and walk through
valleys to get to you.

12.4

[She>]

She's, more. No, she's *much* more.
So much more than a pretty face.
More than a late-night text.
More than a bra, in itty-bitty lace.
More than a skin-tight dress.

She's eloquence. She's freedom.
She's elegance.
She's queendom. She's a diamond.
She's a pearl.
She's all that's right,
in this world.

12.5

[Aura]

There are special places in this universe, among the planets and the stars, high atop the mountains, deep within the seas, and amidst the wilderness. These places contain, what can only be explained, as an aura or chakra—a supernatural presence. Yet no nature, no one, not the Moon nor the Sun is more magical than her.

12.6

[Lighthouse]

She’s my beacon,
my guiding light—the voice that
whispers “Keep going,” when there’s
no end in sight. She’s my daily
reminder to love without compromise,
no matter the consequence.
She’s the reason I now see people
for who they are and for who they
have the potential to be.
She’s the reason I learned to let
live, let love and be free.

12.7

[Two]

Let’s build something strong,
something real—something that’ll
last. A feeling that flows as
fiercely and freely as water rushing
downstream. A bold and unshakable,
unbreakable bond.
Let’s swim with the birds.
Let’s kiss on the moon.
Let’s build a big castle,
a kingdom for two.

12.8

[Illusion]

It's the illusion of choice.
Except, we don't get to choose at
all. Because, '*Once upon a time*'–
next, you've lost your footing.
Suddenly you're falling, faster and
faster. And you've never felt
better. You've given away the keys
to your well-being, your dreams,
and your secrets. You feel free.
Vindicated. Liberated.
Until it dawns on you, those keys
have the power to destroy you.

You take a deep breath, let out a
sigh, and smile, because you
wouldn't have it any other way.

12.9

[Balance]

I choose you, when you doubt,
and can't choose yourself.
You guide me north, when I trip
and lose myself.
I weather your storms and protect
you from rain.
You remedy my heart,
insecurity and pain.
Through deserts, and mountains,
oceans deep or shallow
There's no place I wouldn't go,
as long as you follow.

12.10

[All ways, Always]

It will always be you and I.
I'll float by your side, even when
the sharks swim, with the scent
of your blood.

[Curtains Close]

Inevitably, love will play a role
in your life. Of course, whether
it's the star of the show or a part
of the supporting cast is up to you.
You can live a life of partial,
temporary love, or you can let it
define and consume you in an
unwavering, earth shattering,
overwhelming way. But all there will
ever be, is what's in your heart in
each and every moment, and the
consequences of how you act on it.

Too often, we live lives of lust,
infatuation and mild interest
disguised as love, because the ones
we truly desire seem impossibly out
of reach. We convince ourselves that
we aren't ready, able or deserving.
But we are more than worthy,
of love, passion, romance, and
unrivaled devotion in their many
forms. We need simply to believe
in ourselves wholeheartedly first,
and let the universe take care
of the rest.

If you've ever experienced
heartbreak, find comfort in knowing
you aren't suffering alone.
You won't be hurting forever.
Let the potential for new or
rekindled love heal you and keep
you forever hopeful.

New Era,
Old Love

INSTAGRAM: @SLOAN.SOLARIN

www.ingramcontent.com/pod-product-compliance
Lightning Source LLC
Chambersburg PA
CBHW031623040426
42452CB00007B/640

* 9 7 8 1 7 7 5 1 1 5 4 0 3 *